The
Quotable Dog

The
Quotable Dog

Compiled by
Greg Snider

BARNES
&NOBLE
BOOKS
NEW YORK

For Linda, Marcia, Carol, Lisa, Warren, John, and Budd—each a true dog lover, despite their seven cats

Acknowledgments

━━━━━━━━

My deepest thanks to Linda Gray, whose unending enthusiasm is responsible for this book; to Barry, for the inspiration to try; and to Winston, for eleven years of love, loyalty, and companionship.

Greg Snider

The one absolutely unselfish friend that man can have in this selfish world, the one that never deserts him, the one that never proves ungrateful or treacherous, is his dog.

GEORGE GRAHAM VEST, *EULOGY ON THE DOG*

The reason a dog has so many friends is that he wags his tail instead of his tongue.

ANONYMOUS

I class myself with Rin Tin Tin. At the end of the Depression, people were perhaps looking for something to cheer them up. They fell in love with a dog, and with a little girl.

SHIRLEY TEMPLE, *NEW YORK POST*, 1956

Every boy who has a dog should also have a mother, so the dog can be fed regularly.

ANONYMOUS

Even the tiniest poodle is lionhearted, ready to do anything to defend home, master, and mistress.

LOUIS SABIN, *ALL ABOUT DOGS AS PETS*

What counts is not necessarily the size of the dog in the fight—it's the size of the fight in the dog.

PRESIDENT DWIGHT EISENHOWER

Dogs have given us their absolute all. We are the center of their universe, we are the focus of their love and faith and trust. They serve us in return for scraps. It is without a doubt the best deal man has ever made.

ROGER CARAS, *A CELEBRATION OF DOGS*

Dogs are us, only innocent.

CYNTHIA HEIMEL, *GET YOUR TONGUE OUT OF MY MOUTH, I'M KISSING YOU GOOD-BYE*

A dog is one of the few remaining reasons why some people can be persuaded to go for a walk.

O. A. BATTISTA, *QUOTOONS*

Your pet always thinks you're cool, no matter what brand of shoes you wear. That kind of unconditional love is pretty hard to find. (Just don't slip up and run out of pet munchies or even your dog's loyalty may be tested.)

BRENDA HERRMANN, *CHICAGO TRIBUNE*

I have always thought of a dog lover as a dog that was in love with another dog.

JAMES THURBER

The nose of the bulldog has been slanted backwards so that he can breathe without letting go.

WINSTON CHURCHILL

"We've lost our St. Bernard dog—and it's all mother's fault."

"You mean your mother got lost and you sent the dog out to find her and the dog hasn't come back?"

"No, the dog got lost and we tied a bottle of whisky around mother's neck and sent her out to look for the dog and neither one of them have come back."

MILDRED MEIERS AND JACK KNAPP,
5600 JOKES FOR ALL OCCASIONS

Money will buy a pretty good dog, but it won't buy the wag of his tail.

JOSH BILLINGS

When a dog wags his tail and barks at the same time, how do you know which end to believe?

I wanted a dog to guard the Place and to be a menace to burglars and all that sort of thing. And they've sent us a teddy bear.

ALBERT PAYSON TERHUNE, "THE COMING OF LAD"

Dogs vary as much as their owners vary. Softhearted people have gentle dogs, staid and sober people seem to have glum dogs. Vicious people have vicious dogs and treacherous people treacherous dogs.

IAN NIALL, *ONE MAN AND HIS DOGS*

The dog has seldom pulled man up to his level of sagacity, but man has frequently dragged the dog down to his.

JAMES THURBER

The greatest pleasure of a dog is that you may make a fool of yourself with him, and not only will he not scold you, but he will make a fool of himself, too.

SAMUEL BUTLER

A dog is a man's best friend, and vice versa.

ANONYMOUS

Dogs give their human companions uncon-ditional love and are always there with an encouraging wag of the tail when they are needed. The dog is indeed a very special animal.

DOROTHY HINSHAW PATENT,
DOGS: THE WOLF WITHIN

A dog doesn't care if you're rich or poor, big or small, young or old. He doesn't care if you're not smart, not popular, not a good joke-teller, not the best athlete, not the best-looking person. To your dog, you are the greatest, the smartest, the nicest human being who was ever born. You are his friend and protector.

LOUIS SABIN, *ALL ABOUT DOGS AS PETS*

If you don't own a dog, at least one, there is not necessarily anything wrong with you, but there may be something wrong with your life.

ROGER CARAS, *A CELEBRATION OF DOGS*

A dog teaches a boy fidelity, perseverance, and to turn around three times before lying down.

ROBERT BENCHLEY

Old dogs, like old shoes, are comfortable. They might be a bit out of shape and a little worn around the edges, but they fit well.

BONNIE WILCOX, *OLD DOGS, OLD FRIENDS*

When I was a child, my father told me that when he died he expected to be judged by a panel of Labrador retrievers. I pictured the scene: a semicircle of dogs with stainless steel choke collars and crimson rabies tags. Souls would come forward. The dogs would count sins. The court would be silent, although there might be the jangle of a collar now and then if His Highness, or Her Highness, had a flea.

BENJAMIN H. CHEEVER,
NEW YORK TIMES NEWS SERVICE

I think he understands my business. Unlike any partner I've had, Beau never complains, and he never has asked for a raise.

ALFRED GRIMM, ON HIS POODLE BEAU,
WHO ACCOMPANIES HIM TO WORK
EVERY DAY, CHICAGO TRIBUNE

The dog has got more fun out of man than man has got out of the dog, for man is the more laughable of the two animals.

JAMES THURBER

If you're very wealthy, you ride to hounds; if you're very poor, you go to the dogs.

ANONYMOUS

A reasonable amount o' fleas is good fer a dog—keeps him from brooding over *bein'* a dog.

EDWARD NOYES WESTCOTT, *DAVID HARUM*

A good dog deserves a good bone.

We derive immeasurable good, uncounted pleasures, enormous security, and many critical lessons about life by owning dogs.

ROGER CARAS, *A CELEBRATION OF DOGS*

A watchdog is a dog kept to guard your home, usually by sleeping where a burglar would awaken the household by falling over him.

ANONYMOUS

As an obedience show champion, Hamish . . .
is every dog owner's dream. He fetches and heels
better than the office toady and is usually the
best-behaved passenger when flying to
competitions. If only his owner could stop
Hamish from ordering hotel room service and
movies.

MICHAEL A. LEVINE, ON HAMISH,
A BELGIAN TERVUREN, *CHICAGO TRIBUNE*

There's just something about dogs that makes
you feel good. You come home, they're thrilled
to see you. They're good for the ego.

JANET SCHNELLMAN, THE OWNER OF SANDY,
A YELLOW LABRADOR, *ORLANDO SENTINEL*

He had a terrible, terrible necessity to love, and this trammelled the native, savage hunting beast which he was. He was torn between two great impulses: the native impulse to hunt and kill, and the strange, secondary, supervening impulse to love and obey.

D. H. LAWRENCE, "REX"

Every dog isn't a growler, and every growler isn't a dog.

ANONYMOUS

A dog's bark may be worse than his bite, but everyone prefers his bark.

ANONYMOUS

Every dog is allowed one bite.

PROVERB

The noblest dog of all is the hot dog; it feeds the hand that bites it.

DR. LAURENCE J. PETER

A dog is the only animal that has a love of humans embedded in its DNA.

CYNTHIA HEIMEL, *PLAYBOY*

I could've *sworn* I heard the can opener.

"TOP TEN DOG THOUGHTS," NUMBER 10,
"LATE NIGHT WITH DAVID LETTERMAN"

He could steal and forage to perfection; he had an instinct that was positively gruesome for divining when work was to be done and for making a sneak accordingly; and for getting lost and not staying lost he was nothing short of inspired. But when it came to work, the way that intelligence dribbled out of him and left him a mere clot of wobbling, stupid jelly would make your heart bleed.

JACK LONDON, "THAT SPOT"

Never judge a dog's pedigree by the kind of books he does not chew.

ANONYMOUS

The dog for the man, the cat for the woman.

ENGLISH PROVERB

No matter how little money and how few possessions you own, having a dog makes you rich.

LOUIS SABIN, *ALL ABOUT DOGS AS PETS*

I've wondered why Zachary, my Rin-Tin-Tin look-a-like, has behaved angelically except for the time he took a large bite out of the Laura Ashley chair. Was it a flight of fancy, or does Zak simply have good taste?

DIANE C. ARKINS, *CHICAGO TRIBUNE*

The ideal dog food would be a ration that tastes like a postman.

ANONYMOUS

A dog is a dog except when he is facing you. Then he is Mr. Dog.

HAITIAN FARMER, *NEWSWEEK*

The neighborhood kids had congregated in the front yard when a fire truck zoomed past. Sitting on the front seat was a Boxer dog. The children fell to discussing the dog's duties in connection with the fire truck.

"They use him to keep the crowds back when they go to a fire," said a five-year-old girl.

"No," said another, "they carry him for good luck."

The third, a boy about six, brought the argument to an abrupt end. "They use the dog," he said firmly, "to find the fire plug."

JACOB MORTON BRAUDE,
BRAUDE'S TREASURY OF WIT AND HUMOR

It's a rough-haired canary.

MRS. PAT CAMPBELL, TO A CUSTOMS OFFICER WHO
FOUND HER PET PEKINESE SMUGGLED IN HER MUFF

The deputies thought they were Chihuahuas.

CHIEF OF COOK COUNTY (ILLINOIS)'S
EVICTIONS SECTION, ON AN EVICTION WHERE THE
RATS WERE SO BIG THEY WERE MISTAKEN
FOR DOGS, *CHICAGO TRIBUNE*

I am no mouse! I'm an Asthma Hound
Chihuahua!

BILLY WEST, AS THE VOICE OF REN ON "REN & STIMPY"

Yes, he's got all them different kinds of thoroughbred blood in him, and he's got other kinds you ain't mentioned and that you ain't slick enough to see. You may think you're running him down, but what you say just *proves* he ain't a common dog.

DON MARQUIS, "BLOOD WILL TELL"

The only two who can live as cheaply as one are a dog and a flea.

ANONYMOUS

Between the monster and the fool there are many people who walk the middle path with a dog at their heels, their lives enriched by giving the dog a dog's life.

IAN NIALL, *ONE MAN AND HIS DOGS*

A dog can express more with his tail in minutes than his owner can express with his tongue in hours.

ANONYMOUS

A door is what a dog is always on the wrong side of.

OGDEN NASH, *THE PRIVATE DINING ROOM*

A little attention, a pat on the head, and a kind word every now and then is all [your dog] asks.

LOUIS SABIN, *ALL ABOUT DOGS AS PETS*

I am as confounded by dogs as I am indebted to them.

ROGER CARAS, *A CELEBRATION OF DOGS*

With dogs, you don't need gurus. Dogs are forever in the moment. They are always a tidal wave of feelings, and every feeling is some variant of love.

CYNTHIA HEIMEL, *PLAYBOY*

To his dog, every man is Napoleon, hence the constant popularity of dogs.

ALDOUS HUXLEY

Arfie is a great dog. He wakes up at six A.M. when his human pack leader goes to work, he licks his paws and he goes back to sleep. . . . After dinner, he exists for the hope of some leftovers. Sometimes, he likes to play; the rest of the time, he just likes to exist. . . . Arfie, . . . a constant reminder that life, in general, is no biggie.

JEAN HUARD, *CHICAGO TRIBUNE*

There is only one smartest dog in the world, and every boy has it.

ANONYMOUS

Then who shall picture the urgency of a boy, running, awkwardly, with a great dog in his arms running through the village, past the empty mill, past the Labor Exchange, where the men looked up from their deep ponderings on life and the dole? Or who shall describe the high tones of a voice—a boy's voice, calling as he runs up a path: "Mother! Oh, mother! Lassie's come home! Lassie's come home!"

ERIC KNIGHT, "LASSIE COME-HOME"

The most important role of dogs today is to be our friends and companions. Dogs require loving attention, but they give back more than they receive.

DOROTHY HINSHAW PATENT,
DOGS: THE WOLF WITHIN

You know how such things happen: One is taking a walk, and then—there's a lost dog in your tracks. You think, Hey, what's this tagging along? You raise your hand to the dog and shout, "Beat it!" The dog stops, bows like a human, and just as you're trying to smack him one, manages to get even closer. Now you bend, you make a feint with your hand, pretending to throw a rock at him. It does no good. You stand watching the dog; the dog stands watching you. You look silently into each other's eyes. . . .

That's the kind of dog our Rabchik was.

SHALOM ALEICHEM, "RABCHIK, A JEWISH DOG"

You always sympathize with the underdog, except when the other dog is yours.

ANONYMOUS

"Your dog likes to watch you cut hair, doesn't he?"

"It ain't that. Sometimes I snip off a bit of ear."

JACOB MORTON BRAUDE, RECOUNTING A BARBER-SHOP CONVERSATION, *BRAUDE'S TREASURY OF WIT AND HUMOR*

Among the excuses I have yet to hear, but wouldn't be surprised to hear soon: "The dog ate my deposit slips."

CLARENCE PAGE, ON THE U.S. HOUSE BANKING SCANDAL, *CHICAGO TRIBUNE*

Q. Why does a dog hang his tongue out of his mouth?

A. To balance his tail.

MILDRED MEIERS AND JACK KNAPP, *5600 JOKES FOR ALL OCCASIONS*

There was an air of majesty, of perfect breeding, about Bruce—an intangible something that lent him the bearing of a monarch.

ALBERT PAYSON TERHUNE, "YOUTH WILL BE SERVED!"

He seemed neither old nor young. His strength lay in his eyes. They looked as old as the hills, and as young and as wild. I never tired looking into them.

JOHN MUIR, "AN ADVENTURE WITH A DOG"

Every dog may have his day, but it's the puppies that have the weak ends.

ANONYMOUS

Nipper's like any other actor—at work he's got a serious personality. But when you open the door to his suite, he takes off a hundred miles per hour.

BARBARA AUSTIN, OWNER OF THE DAWN ANIMAL AGENCY, ON NIPPER, RCA'S FAMOUS JACK RUSSELL TERRIER

Even the tiniest poodle or Chihuahua is still a wolf at heart.

DOROTHY HINSHAW PATENT, *DOGS: THE WOLF WITHIN*

I'm a lean dog, a keen dog, a wild dog, and
    alone;
I'm a rough dog, a tough dog, hunting on my
    own;
I'm a bad dog, a mad dog, teasing silly sheep;
I love to sit and bay at the moon, to keep fat
    souls from sleep.

IRENE RUTHERFORD MCLEOD, "THE LONE DOG"

"Say, what's the matter with that dog of yours?
Every time I come near the water cooler, he
growls."

"Oh, he won't bother you."

"Then what's he growling about?"

"He's probably a little sore because you're
drinking out of his cup."

MILDRED MEIERS AND JACK KNAPP,
5600 JOKES FOR ALL OCCASIONS

My father was a Saint Bernard, my mother was a collie, but I am a Presbyterian.

MARK TWAIN, "A DOG'S TALE"

Here one day would stand a giant among dogs, powerful as a timber wolf, lithe as a cat, as dangerous to foes as an angry tiger; a dog without fear or treachery; a dog of uncanny brain and great lovingly loyal heart and, withal, a dancing sense of fun. A dog with a soul.

ALBERT PAYSON TERHUNE, "THE COMING OF LAD"

One reason a dog is such a comfort when you're downcast is that he doesn't ask to know why.

ANONYMOUS

Buy a pup and your money will buy
Love unflinching that cannot lie.

RUDYARD KIPLING

A dog gladly admits the superiority of his master over himself, accepts his judgment as final, but, contrary to what many dog-lovers believe, he does not consider himself a slave. His submission is voluntary, and he expects his own small rights to be respected.

AXEL MUNTHE, *THE STORY OF SAN MICHELE*

When some men go to the dogs, it's pretty tough on the dogs.

ANONYMOUS

Girl: Here Broker, here Broker!
Man: Oh, is your dog on the stock market?
Girl: No, he does his trading on the curb.

MILDRED MEIERS AND JACK KNAPP,
5600 JOKES FOR ALL OCCASIONS

When you have dogs for a long time and keep them for the quality they have that is quite beyond compromise, you make many treaties that are hard to keep.

DION HENDERSON, "BROKEN TREATY"

Every man gets mad when a dog bites him, whether the dog is mad or not.

ANONYMOUS

He was always sorry, mother said, after he bit someone, but we could not understand how she figured this out. He didn't act sorry.

JAMES THURBER, *THE DOG THAT BIT PEOPLE*

Every boy should have two things: a dog, and a mother willing to let him have one.

ANONYMOUS

His was the collie heritage—the stark need for comradeship coupled with the unconscious craving to be owned by man and to give his devotion to man, his god.

ALBERT PAYSON TERHUNE, "FOX!"

At times it was like gazing into a human soul, to look into his eyes; and what I saw there frightened me and started all sorts of ideas in my own mind of reincarnation and all the rest. I tell you I sensed something big in that brute's eyes; there was a message there, but I wasn't big enough myself to catch it.

JACK LONDON, "THAT SPOT"

The dog is all things to all men.

IAN NIALL, *ONE MAN AND HIS DOGS*

Animals are such agreeable friends—they ask no questions, they pass no criticisms.

GEORGE ELIOT

It's no coincidence that man's best friend cannot talk.

ANONYMOUS

It follows not, because
The hair is rough, the dog's a savage one.

J. SHERIDAN KNOWLES, "THE DAUGHTER"

Play safe: let sleeping dogs lie, and let lying dogs sleep.

ANONYMOUS

The person had only to stop and smile, and Attila would melt. He would behave as if he apologized for even giving an impression of violence. He would lower his head, curve his body, tuck his tail between his legs, roll his eyes and moan as if to say, "How sad that you should have mistaken my gesture! I only hurried down to greet you."

R. K. NARAYAN, *MALGUDI DAYS*

A dog's bark may be worse than his bite, but it's never quite so personal.

ANONYMOUS

The more I see of men, the more I like dogs.

MME. DE STAËL

When the old kennel hands begin to talk of memorable dogs, one of the things they remember best is the royal manner—the flashing stride, the relentless courage, the flare of style, and the champion's heart. Such dogs do not always achieve royal standing in the world of dog competitions because they do not always have the chance, but when they do, they know that they do, and they are as proud as a man of the achievement.

DION HENDERSON, "BROKEN TREATY"

No breeder is above catering to intelligent praise of his dog.

ALBERT PAYSON TERHUNE, "LOCHINVAR BOBBY"

The woman who is really kind to dogs is always one who has failed to inspire sympathy in men.

MAX BEERBOHM, *ZULEIKA DOBSON*

If a dachshund's head you pat on Sunday, he'll wag his little tail on Monday.

ANONYMOUS

There are two kinds of fidelity, that of dogs and that of cats: you, gentlemen, have the fidelity of cats, who never leave the house.

NAPOLEON BONAPARTE, SPEAKING AFTER HE HAD ESCAPED FROM ELBA, TO FRENCH COURTIERS WHO HAD NOT FOLLOWED HIM THERE

A dog knows his master, a cat does not.

ELEAZAR B. ZADOK

No man can be condemned for owning a dog. As long as he has a dog, he has a friend; and the poorer he gets, the better friend he has.

WILL ROGERS

Dogs laugh, but they laugh with their tails.

MAX EASTMAN

If a dog could talk, he wouldn't long remain man's best friend.

ANONYMOUS

Humans were denied the speech of animals. The only common ground of communication upon which dogs and men can get together is in fiction.

O. HENRY, "MEMOIRS OF A YELLOW DOG"

If you pick up a starving dog and make him prosperous, he will not bite you. That is the principal difference between a dog and a man.

MARK TWAIN, *PUDD'NHEAD WILSON'S CALENDAR*

Barking dogs don't bite, but they themselves don't know it.

SHALOM ALEICHEM

Show a dog a finger, and he wants the whole hand.

YIDDISH PROVERB

Killing the dog does not cure the bite.

ANONYMOUS

It doesn't take intelligence to make a dog run when he sees a gun, but Fluff did not run like an ordinary dog. He saw the gun and he saw the ducks, and he saw that Brownlee only shot at ducks when they were on the wing. And he thought Brownlee meant to shoot him, so what does he do? Stand still? No; he tries to fly.

ELLIS PARKER BUTLER, "GETTING RID OF FLUFF"

The censure of a dog is something no man can stand.

CHRISTOPHER MORLEY, *THE HAUNTED BOOKSHOP*

We are all in the same boat, both animals and men. You cannot promote kindness to one without benefiting the other.

EDWARD EVERETT HALE

My little old dog:
A heart-beat At my feet.

EDITH WHARTON, *A LYRICAL EPIGRAM*

Folk will know how large your soul is,
  By the way you treat a dog!

CHARLES F. DORAN

The worst dog gets the best bone.

PERETZ

My feeling toward the animal is that he is our younger brother, and that we *are* our brother's keeper.

MARY JOHNSTON

My dog! the difference between thee and me
Knows only our Creator.

LAMARTINE

Scratch a dog and you'll find a permanent job.

FRANKLIN P. JONES

Don't make the mistake of treating your dogs like humans, or they'll treat you like dogs.

MARTHA SCOTT

I always thought that my canine family tended to view me as the funny-looking two-legged dog who runs the can opener.

ROGER CARAS, *A DOG IS LISTENING*

Stick around any place long enough and chances are you'll be taken for granted. Hang around for 20,000 years wagging your tail and being man's (and woman's) best friend, and you'll be taken for granted big time.

LYNN VAN MATRE, *CHICAGO TRIBUNE*

Dogs, like human infants, learn by imitation. *Show* him what you want; whether or not he performs, he will be duly amused by your hilarious attempts to please him.

STEPHEN BAKER, *HOW TO LIVE WITH A NEUROTIC DOG*

I can train any dog in five minutes. It's training the owner that takes longer.

BARBARA WOODHOUSE

"Is he a good watch dog?"

"Rather. If you hear a suspicious noise at night you have only to wake him and he begins to bark."

MILDRED MEIERS AND JACK KNAPP,
5600 JOKES FOR ALL OCCASIONS

When a puppy takes fifty catnaps in the course of the day, he cannot always be expected to sleep the night through. It is too much to ask.

ALBERT PAYSON TERHUNE, "THE COMING OF LAD"

It is a terrible thing for an old lady to outlive her dogs.

TENNESSEE WILLIAMS, *CAMINO REAL*

Histories are more full of examples of the fidelity of dogs than of friends.

ALEXANDER POPE

To be sure, the dog is loyal. But why, on that account, should we take him as an example? He is loyal to men, not to other dogs.

KARL KRAUS

If your home burns down, rescue the dogs. At least they'll be faithful to you.

LEE MARVIN

Brother and sisters, I bid you beware
Of giving your heart to a dog to tear.

RUDYARD KIPLING, "THE POWER OF THE DOG"

Dog. A kind of additional or subsidiary Deity
designed to catch the overflow and surplus of
the world's worship.

AMBROSE BIERCE

A dog is the only thing on earth that loves you
more than you love yourself.

JOSH BILLINGS

Eric: He's lovely dog . . . Last Saturday he took first prize at the cat show.
Ernie: How was that?
Eric: He took the cat.

ERIC MORECAMBE AND ERNIE WISE,
THE MORECAMBE AND WISE JOKE BOOK

Well-washed and well-combed domestic pets grow dull; they miss the stimulus of fleas.

FRANCIS GALTON

America is a very large, friendly dog in a very small room. Every time it wags its tail it knocks over a chair.

ARNOLD TOYNBEE

Near this spot
Are deposited the remains of one
Who possessed Beauty without Vanity
Strength without Insolence
Courage without Ferocity
And all the Virtues of Man without his Vices.
This Praise, which would be unmeaning Flattery
If inscribed over human ashes,
Is but a just tribute to the Memory of
   BOATSWAIN, a Dog.

LORD BYRON'S INSCRIPTION ON THE
TOMB OF HIS DOG, 1808

Why keep a dog and bark yourself?

PROVERB

The usual dog about the Town
Is much inclined to play the clown.

T. S. ELIOT, "OLD POSSUM'S
BOOK OF PRACTICAL CATS"

When we first found out that Comet had
gotten a feature, we were all resentful. But now
I've decided to kiss up to him.

ACTOR BOB SAGET, ON COMET,
THE GOLDEN RETRIEVER FEATURED IN THE
TELEVISION SHOW "FULL HOUSE," TV GUIDE

It has taken me years to realize the greatness of
a dog.

ZANE GREY, "DON"

It is a strange thing, love. Nothing but love has made the dog lose his wild freedom, to become the servant of man. And this very servility or completeness of love makes him a term of deepest contempt—"You dog!"

D. H. LAWRENCE, "REX"

Let dogs delight to bark and bite
For God hath made them so.

ISAAC WATTS, "DIVINE SONGS FOR CHILDREN"

I have caught more ills from people sneezing over me and giving me virus infections than from kissing dogs.

BARBARA WOODHOUSE,
TELEGRAPH SUNDAY MAGAZINE

Say something idiotic and nobody but a dog politely wags his tail.

VIRGINIA GRAHAM, *EVERYTHING'S TOO SOMETHING*

Asking a working writer what he thinks about critics is like asking a lamp-post how it feels about dogs.

CHRISTOPHER HAMPTON, THE *SUNDAY NEW YORK TIMES MAGAZINE*

The relationship between man and dog can often be as complex as that between man and woman. We have, own, or are owned by dogs for a great variety of reasons, not all of them exactly to our credit.

IAN NIALL, *ONE MAN AND HIS DOGS*

Regardless of what they say about it, we are going to keep it.

**RICHARD NIXON, REFERRING TO CHECKERS,
A DOG GIVEN TO THE NIXON CHILDREN,
WHILE DEFENDING HIMSELF AGAINST
CORRUPTION CHARGES**

He's SMALL.
He's BLACK.
He's MAD AS HELL.
He's POODLE with a MOHAWK.
You'll never call him Fifi again!

LYNDA BARRY

Every day, the dog and I, we go for a tramp in the woods. And he loves it! Mind you, the tramp is getting a bit fed up!

JERRY DENNIS

A dog with money is addressed as "Mr. Dog."

SPANISH PROVERB

It's a dog-eat-dog world . . . and I'm wearing Milk-Bone underwear.

T-SHIRT SLOGAN

You think dogs will not be in heaven? I tell you, they will be there long before any of us.

ROBERT LOUIS STEVENSON

Politics are not my concern . . . they impressed me as a dog's life without a dog's decencies.

RUDYARD KIPLING, *A DIVERSITY OF CREATURES*

Generally, or at least very often, people with a deep interest in animals are the best people around.

ROGER CARAS, *A DOG IS LISTENING*

You can't keep a good man down—or an overaffectionate dog.

ANONYMOUS

MAN'S BEST FRIEND, only better! No smudges on car windows. Frisbees come back dry. Won't drink from toilet, sniff your friends, or chew up your favorite sneakers. Much better kisses.

FROM A PERSONALS ADVERTISEMENT
IN THE *READER*, CHICAGO

I wonder if other dogs think poodles are members of a weird religious cult.

RITA RUDNER

There is no greater pleasure than having a dog. And that's a scientific fact!

LOUIS SABIN, COMMENTING ON A UNIVERSITY STUDY ON THE EFFECT OF OWNING A DOG, *ALL ABOUT DOGS AS PETS*

No animal I know of can consistently be more of a friend and companion than a dog.

STANLEY LEINWOLL, *THE BOOK OF PETS*

It doesn't matter where you are in your own personal development, nor has it mattered where you have been culturally; dogs simply don't pass judgment on you the way all of the rest of life and all of your other companions seem to.

ROGER CARAS, *A CELEBRATION OF DOGS*

Toddy: I'm naturally warm-blooded.
Victoria: To be *that* warm blooded you'd have to be a St. Bernard!

ROBERT PRESTON (TODDY), DENYING HIS HIGH FEVER TO JULIE ANDREWS (VICTORIA) IN *VICTOR/VICTORIA*

To bark when he's in danger, to run and play with him when he's happy, to nuzzle him when he's lonely: That's why they call us man's best friend.

DON AMECHE, AS THE VOICE OF SHADOW, A WISE OLD GOLDEN RETRIEVER IN *HOMEWARD BOUND*

Dogs and humans are symbiotic species. We need each other.

CYNTHIA HEIMEL, *PLAYBOY*

When most of us talk to our dogs, we tend to forget they're not people.

JULIA GLASS, *REDBOOK*

The dog was created specially for children. He is the god of frolic.

HENRY WARD BEECHER

You own a dog; you feed a cat.

JIM FIEBIG

It don't care whether I'm good enough. It don't care whether I snore or not. It don't care which God I pray to. There are only three things in this world with that kind of unconditional acceptance: Dogs, donuts, and money.

DANNY DEVITO, AS LAWRENCE GARFIELD,
IN *OTHER PEOPLE'S MONEY*

Flatterers look like friends, as wolves like dogs.

GEORGE CHAPMAN

There is no psychiatrist in the world like a
puppy licking your face.

BERN WILLIAMS

His puppyhood was a period of foolish
rebellion. He was always worsted, but he fought
back because it was his nature to fight back.
And he was unconquerable.

JACK LONDON, "BÂTARD"

Don't accept your dog's admiration as conclusive evidence that you are wonderful.

ANN LANDERS

If dogs could talk, it would take a lot of fun out of owning one.

ANDY ROONEY, *NOT THAT YOU ASKED . . .*

Cute puppies and eternal glory. Add a splash of sex and you've got the essence of the American Dream.

JACK BARTH, *AMERICAN QUEST*

He was never on a leash, not even in New York City. He would walk with you to the corner, wait for you to cross the street, then trot along beside you. He would wait outside of stores for you while you shopped. He was also extremely friendly and just generally had a kind of existential, world-weary air to him that made you believe he was capable of carrying on a very interesting drawing room conversation. In French.

PETER GETHERS, REFLECTING ON HIS BROTHER'S COCKAPOO, YOSSARIAN, IN *THE CAT WHO WENT TO PARIS*

Any time you think you have influence, try ordering around someone else's dog.

THE COCKLE BUR

When a dog runs at you, whistle for him.

HENRY DAVID THOREAU

"I want a dog of which I can be proud," said Mrs. Newlyrich. "Does that one have a good pedigree?"

"Oh, yes," declared the kennel owner, "if he could talk, he wouldn't speak to either of us."

JACOB MORTON BRAUDE,
BRAUDE'S TREASURY OF WIT AND HUMOR

Personality is what a man has if his dog starts running for him the moment he comes into sight.

O. A. BATTISTA, QUOTOONS

Even a blind dog finds a bone once in a while.

FORMER SAN FRANCISCO GIANTS PITCHER
MIKE KRUKOW, ON DRIVING IN A WINNING RUN

Having a dog means that the child inside
yourself is made manifest in canine form.

CYNTHIA HEIMEL, *GET YOUR TONGUE OUT OF MY
MOUTH, I'M KISSING YOU GOOD-BYE*

A beautiful experience.

PRESIDENT GEORGE BUSH ON HIS DOG
MILLIE'S GETTING PREGNANT

Super-intelligent dogs that really can play poker so you could just photograph them instead of buying one of those fancy novelty paintings.

I explained it to St. Peter,
I'd rather stay here,
Outside the pearly gate.
I won't be a nuisance,
I won't even bark,
I'll be very patient and wait.
I'll be here, chewing on a celestial bone,
No matter how long you may be.
I'd miss you so much, if I went in alone,
It wouldn't be heaven for me.

ANONYMOUS

If you can't run with the big dogs, stay on the porch.

It wouldn't be right. It's embarrassing for a hunter to get shot by a dog.

He who lies down with dogs gets up with fleas.

There are three faithful friends—an old wife, an old dog, and ready money.

BENJAMIN FRANKLIN

How to recognize Germans: Their grass is always perfect, and both their dogs and their children have been trained to heel.

JOHN LOUIS ANDERSON,
GERMAN HUMOR: ON THE FRITZ

My husband and I are either going to buy a dog or have a child. We can't decide whether to ruin our carpets or ruin our lives.

RITA RUDNER

If the old dog hadn't got distracted by the fire plug, he would have caught the rabbit.

HAYES MCCLERKIN, ON ROSS PEROT'S LOSING DIRECTION IN THE 1992 PRESIDENTIAL CAMPAIGN

I'm worried about Vladimir standing there in the gutter.

A PARISIAN, ON BEING FORCED BY NEW LITTER LAWS TO CURB HER DOG

Who goes looting with their dog?

A LOS ANGELES RESIDENT, BAILING OUT HIS HOUSEKEEPER, WHO WAS CHARGED WITH LOOTING WHILE INNOCENTLY WALKING HER DOG DURING THE 1993 LOS ANGELES RIOTS

Sometimes you panic and find yourself emitting remarks so profoundly inane that you would be embarrassed to say them to your dog. Your dog would look at you and think to itself, "I may lick myself in public, but I'd never say anything as stupid as that."

DAVE BARRY

They wanted a dog who could melt into a chair.

ANIMAL TRAINER BETTY LINN, ON MAUI, THE DOG WHO PLAYS MURRAY ON TELEVISION'S "MAD ABOUT YOU"

I built him a doghouse here, but he ate it.

OWNER OF A DOG-WOLF HYBRID

My views of him are similar to those of a fire hydrant toward dogs.

SPEAKER OF THE HOUSE JIM WRIGHT, IN 1988, ON THE MOVE BY REPRESENTATIVE NEWT GINGRICH TO HAVE HIM INVESTIGATED FOR POSSIBLE UNETHICAL BEHAVIOR

This is sort of apropos.

A MARYLAND VOTER, ON BEING ASKED HIS VIEWS ON PRESIDENTIAL POLITICS WHILE CLEANING UP DOG EXCREMENT FROM HIS SIDEWALK

Dogs remember faces; cats, places.

ENGLISH SAYING

The cat is the mirror of his human's mind . . . the dog mirrors his human's physical appearance.

WINIFRED CARRIERE

Sometimes in the NBA, you feel like a dog. You age seven years in one.

FRANK LAYDEN, ON RESIGNING AS COACH OF THE NBA'S UTAH JAZZ

A lawyer is just like an attack dog, only without a conscience.

TOM CLANCY

She plans to retire to her cabin in New Hampshire, get a dog—she's always wanted a dog—continue writing and working for the rights of the children of inmates.

ATTORNEY MICHAEL KENNEDY ON JEAN HARRIS'S
PLANS AFTER HER RELEASE FROM PRISON

Poopsie is no spring chicken either.

FRANCINE GLOBECK, 59, ON PARTICIPATING WITH
HER DACHSHUND IN A STEEPLECHASE
FOR DOGS AND OWNERS

I sometimes look into the face of my dog Stan and see wistful sadness and existential angst when all he is actually doing is slowly scanning the ceiling for flies.

MERRILL MARKOE, *WHAT THE DOGS HAVE TAUGHT ME*

Possibly disillusioning data about some of your favorite cinematic canines:
• Rin Tin Tin was named for a French charm.
• Disney's "Shaggy Dog" was bought for $2 at a pound.
• Old Yeller was bought for $3 from a shelter; his real name was Spike.

WORLD FEATURES SYNDICATE

I once decided not to date a guy because he wasn't excited to meet my dog. I mean, this was like not wanting to meet my mother.

BONNIE SCHACHTER, FOUNDER OF THE SINGLE PET OWNERS' SOCIETY SINGLES GROUP, *LOS ANGELES DAILY NEWS*

1. Justice and Order

2. Dogs

NUMBERS 1 AND 2 ON EDITH WHARTON'S
LIST OF "RULING PASSIONS"

Houses are for private living, for friends, and for dogs.

FRANÇOISE SAGAN

Diamonds are a girl's best friend. Dogs are a man's best friend. Now you know which sex is smarter.

NANCY GRAY, *STUPID MEN JOKES*

My dogs are my children.

ST. LOUIS RESIDENT CARLA JULIUS, SEEKING
CUSTODY OF HER DOGS IN HER DIVORCE HEARING

. . . divided custody, with the provision that the dog "not be allowed to associate with ill-bred animals and that it not be allowed to drink any alcoholic beverages."

A JUDGMENT IN A PULASKI, TENNESSEE,
DIVORCE COURT REGARDING ARISTOTLE, THE
COUPLE'S DOG, NEW YORK TIMES NEWS SERVICE

People can be a fine substitute for other dogs. But I think that if they had to choose, dogs by and large would choose the company of other dogs.

ANTHROPOLOGIST ELIZABETH MARSHALL THOMAS,
THE HIDDEN LIFE OF DOGS

My name is Oprah Winfrey. I have a talk show. I'm single. I have eight dogs—five golden retrievers, two black labs, and a mongrel. I have four years of college.

OPRAH WINFREY, IN A CHICAGO FEDERAL COURTROOM, RESPONDING TO A REQUEST FOR POTENTIAL JURORS TO DESCRIBE THEMSELVES

. . . none are as fiercely loyal as dog people. In return, no doubt, for the never-ending loyalty of dogs.

LINDA SHRIEVES, *ORLANDO SENTINEL*

A few mornings ago, on the way to work, we noticed a woman letting her poodle sip coffee from a cup. "Is that good for the dog?" we asked. "Of course," said the woman. "But she'll only drink French roast."

RICK KOGAN, *CHICAGO TRIBUNE*

Maintain a discreet distance from two-legged friends when riding in elevators.

FROM THE "CANINE CODE OF BEHAVIOR" SIGN IN CHICAGO'S AMBASSADOR EAST HOTEL

The dog had lunch with the corner of it.

DAVID SCHENKEL, ORGANIZER OF THE QUAYLE CENTER AND MUSEUM, ON THE FORMER VICE PRESIDENT'S INDIANA UNIVERSITY LAW DEGREE, WHICH SPORTS EXTENSIVE CHEW MARKS

Whoever beats dog loves not man.

ARSÈNE HOUSSAYE

My dog Millie knows more about foreign affairs than these two bozos.

PRESIDENT GEORGE BUSH, REFERRING TO BILL CLINTON AND AL GORE DURING A CAMPAIGN SPEECH IN WARREN, MICHIGAN

Like all celebrities, they've got a routine when on the road: first-class seat (always right side, second row, window), a stretch limo waiting, the finest in hotel suites and Evian water.

TODD COPILEVITZ, *DALLAS MORNING NEWS*, ON RCA'S FAMOUS JACK RUSSELL TERRIERS NIPPER AND CHIPPER

When a man's dog turns against him it is time for his wife to pack her trunk and go home to mamma.

MARK TWAIN

I wanted a child, and he is my child. . . . Oh, and he has to be covered up at night, or he won't go to sleep.

THE OWNER OF MO, A SEVEN-YEAR-OLD DALMATIAN, KNIGHT-RIDDER NEWSPAPERS

Recollect that the Almighty, who gave the dog to be companion of our pleasures and our toils, hath invested him with a nature noble and incapable of deceit.

SIR WALTER SCOTT

The poor dog, in life the firmest friend,
The first to welcome, foremost to defend.

LORD BYRON

Happiness is a warm puppy.

CHARLES SCHULZ

Happiness isn't a warm puppy—it's a big,
slobbery Saint Bernard.

FROM AN *ENTERTAINMENT WEEKLY*
REVIEW OF THE MOVIE *BEETHOVEN*

It sounds like something the English would do.

ROLANDO TUCCI, A RESIDENT OF AREZZO, ITALY,
ON A PLAN TO DISTRIBUTE UNDERPANTS FOR DOGS
IN AN EFFORT TO KEEP LOCAL SIDEWALKS
CLEAN, *NEWSWEEK*

Heaven goes by favor. If it went by merit, you would stay out and your dog would go in.

MARK TWAIN

A collie has the brain of a man, and the ways of a woman.

SCOTTISH PROVERB

Friends and relatives who once shook their heads at my intolerance for dogs now giggle at my "spoiling" Buster. Severely untrue! Okay, I hold ice-cream cones while Buster licks them or hand-feed him ice chips in hot weather because they slip and slide in his bowl: *Buster has no hands*!

LARRY L. KING, *PARADE* MAGAZINE

Mistaken in assumption there would be chance to show off talent for drinking from toilet.

"TOP TEN DOG EXCUSES FOR LOSING THE DOG SHOW," NUMBER 10, "LATE NIGHT WITH DAVID LETTERMAN"

You may have a dog that won't sit up, roll over or even cook breakfast, not because he's too stupid to learn how but because he's too smart to bother.

RICK HOROWITZ, *CHICAGO TRIBUNE*

A perfect fashion accessory.

STANLEY COREN, AUTHOR OF *THE INTELLIGENCE OF DOGS*, ON THE LOWEST-RANKED OF 133 BREEDS, THE AFGHAN

"Well, well, what a cute pup. Is he a bird dog?"
"Sure. Here, Fido, give the lady the bird."

MILDRED MEIERS AND JACK KNAPP, *5600 JOKES FOR ALL OCCASIONS*

It was odd to see her as she watched the man, my father, crouching and talking to the little dog and laughing strangely when the little creature bit his nose and toused his beard. What does a woman think of her husband at such a moment?

D. H. LAWRENCE, "REX"

Every dog has its day, and I have had mine.

GEORGE BERNARD SHAW

There are no one-night stands with a dog. Once you let your pet into your bed, it's hard to get him out.

DIANA DELMAR, *THE GUILT-FREE DOG OWNER'S GUIDE*

Ring honors usually come in youth or not at all. Yes, and they depart with youth. The dog remains handsome and useful for years thereafter. But his head has coarsened. His figure has lost its perfection. His gait stiffens. In a score of ways he drops back from the standard required of winners. Younger dogs are put above him. And that is life—whether in kennel, or in stable, or in office, or in the courts of love. Youth wins.

ALBERT PAYSON TERHUNE, "YOUTH WILL BE SERVED!"

Other men saw to the welfare of their dogs from a sense of duty and business expediency; he saw to the welfare of his as if they were his own children, because he could not help it.

JACK LONDON, "FOR THE LOVE OF A MAN"

A man and his dog goes so well with home and castle.

IAN NIALL, *ONE MAN AND HIS DOGS*

The great dog raised himself, and placing his forepaws on his master's chest tenderly, lest he should hurt him who was already hurt past healing, stood towering above him; while the little man laid his two cold hands on the dog's shoulders.

So they stood, looking at one another, like a man and his love.

ALFRED OLLIVANT, "THE TAILLESS TYKE AT BAY"

We called him Old Yeller. The name had a sort of double meaning. One part meant that his short hair was a dingy yellow, a color that we called "yeller" in those days. The other meant that when he opened his head, the sound he let out came closer to being a yell than a bark.

FRED GIPSON, *OLD YELLER*

You do not have to strike your dog for doing wrong. Your frowns, finger shakes, and sharp words are enough.

JEAN CRAIGHEAD GEORGE,
HOW TO TALK TO YOUR DOG

The small percentage of dogs that bite people is monumental proof that the dog is the most benign, forgiving creature on earth.

W. R. KOEHLER, *THE KOEHLER METHOD OF DOG TRAINING*

All knowledge, the totality of all questions and all answers, is contained in the dog.

FRANZ KAFKA, "INVESTIGATIONS OF A DOG"

I cannot impress on my readers too strongly the necessity to be firm but kind to a puppy. His idea of your authority is forming, and if he knows you give in on the slightest whimper, you are whacked for life.

BARBARA WOODHOUSE, *DOG TRAINING MY WAY*

I own two dogs, and they both have been trained to respond immediately to my voice. For example, when we're outside, all I have to do is issue the following standard dog command: "Here Earnest! Here Zippy! C'mon! Here! I said come HERE! You dogs COME HERE RIGHT NOW! ARE YOU DOGS LISTENING TO ME? HEY!!!" And instantly both dogs, in unison, like a precision drill team, will continue trotting in random directions, sniffing the ground.

DAVE BARRY, "YELLOW JOURNALISM"

Of all the dogs whom I have served I've never known one who understood so much of what I say or held it in such deep contempt.

E. B. WHITE, "DOG TRAINING"

Dogs love to roll in obnoxious organic material because they have a highly evolved sense of smell, probably a million times better than ours, and I believe that they have an esthetic sense in this modality: they like to wear odors much as we, a more visually oriented species, like to wear bright clothes or something different for a while.

MICHAEL W. FOX, *SUPERDOG: RAISING THE PERFECT CANINE COMPANION*

There's facts about dogs, and there's opinions about them. The dogs have the facts, and the humans have the opinions. If you want facts about a dog, always get them straight from the dog. If you want opinions, get them from humans.

J. ALLEN BOONE, *KINSHIP WITH ALL LIFE*

Many dogs will give a greeting grin much like a human smile.

RICHARD A. WOLTERS, *HOME DOG*

Dogs aren't born knowing what or what not to do; they only learn like children.

BARBARA WOODHOUSE, *NO BAD DOGS, THE WOODHOUSE WAY*

The training of the dog is something which should be left to the boy, as this teaches him responsibility and accustoms him to the use of authority, probably the only time he will ever have a chance to use it.

ROBERT BENCHLEY, "YOUR BOY AND HIS DOG"

Humans have externalized their wisdom— stored it in museums, libraries, the expertise of the learned. Dog wisdom is inside the blood and bones.

DONALD MCCAIG, *NOP'S TRIALS*

The fidelity of a dog is a precious gift demanding no less binding moral responsibilities than the friendship of a human being. The bond with a true dog is as lasting as the ties of this earth can ever be.

KONRAD LORENZ, *MAN MEETS DOG*

Show dogs have been bred to live off the fat of the land. The only feathers they've ever seen were on the hat of some female judge.

RICHARD A. WOLTERS, *GUN DOG*

Dogs understand your moods and your thoughts, and if you are thinking unpleasant things about your dog, he will pick it up and be downhearted.

BARBARA WOODHOUSE, *NO BAD DOGS,*
THE WOODHOUSE WAY

We had called the dog Stranger out of the faint hope that he was just passing through. As it turned out, the name was most inappropriate since he stayed on for nearly a score of years, all the while biting the hands that fed him and making snide remarks about my grandmother's cooking. Eventually the name was abbreviated to "Strange," which was shorter and much more descriptive.

PATRICK F. MCMANUS, "A DOG FOR ALL SEASONS"

The famed brandy cask is a myth. It probably began due to the fact that the lost traveler, once found, was usually offered brandy by the [Augustinian] Brother who accompanied the search dog. But the Brother carried the brandy, not the dog.

THE MONKS OF NEW SKETE, *HOW TO BE YOUR DOG'S BEST FRIEND*

Personal friendship means everything to a dog; but remember, it entails no small responsibility, for a dog is not a servant to whom you can easily give notice. And remember, too, if you are an over-sensitive person, that the life of your friend is much shorter than your own and a sad parting, after ten or fifteen years, is inevitable.

KONRAD LORENZ, *KING SOLOMON'S RING*

The prospective buyer sits in the middle of the litter and plays with all the pups. The one that pulls at his cuff, pounces through the pack, climbs up into his lap, and paws at his shirt to give him a love lick is usually the one that wins his heart and gets bed and board for life.

RICHARD A. WOLTERS, *GAME DOG*

I realized clearly, perhaps for the first time, what strained and anxious lives dogs must lead, so emotionally involved in the world of men, whose affections they strive endlessly to secure, whose authority they are expected unquestioningly to obey, and whose mind they never can do more than imperfectly reach and comprehend.

J. R. ACKERLEY, *MY DOG TULIP*

Intelligent dogs rarely want to please people whom they do not respect.

W. R. KOEHLER, *THE KOEHLER METHOD OF DOG TRAINING*

When you point out something to a dog, he looks at your finger.

J. BRYAN III, *HODGEPODGE TWO*

I do not believe in paying off a dog by shoving food into his mouth every time he does something he was bred to do. I like to think that the training is taking place in the head, not the stomach. A kind word in his ear is making the brain work; food in the stomach only makes the bowels work.

RICHARD A. WOLTERS, *GUN DOG*

When training a dog, it is important to leave it wanting to do more. In other words, train your dog until it is tired; you want your dog to *want* to work, not to *have* to work.

JANET RUCKERT, *ARE YOU MY DOG?*

Never repeat a command. Most dogs are not deaf; they just choose not to listen.

CONNIE JANKOWSKI WITH LAURIE RUBENFELD, "PUPPY TRAINING SECRETS"

The dog wags its tail only at living things. A tail wag, the equivalent of a human smile, is bestowed upon people, dogs, cats, squirrels, even mice and butterflies—but no lifeless things. A dog won't wag its tail to its dinner or to a bed, car, stick, or even a bone.

JEAN CRAIGHEAD GEORGE,
HOW TO TALK TO YOUR DOG

Dogs read the world through their noses and write their history in urine.

J. R. ACKERLEY, *MY DOG TULIP*

He may be a dog, but don't tell me he doesn't have a real grip on life.

KENDALL HAILEY, *THE DAY I BECAME AN AUTODIDACT*

You didn't have to throw a stick in the water to get him to go in. Of course, he would bring back a stick if you did throw one in. He would even have brought back a piano if you had thrown one in.

JAMES THURBER, "SNAPSHOT OF A DOG"

He was born in Bercy on the outskirts of Paris and trained in France, and while he knows a little poodle-English, he responds quickly only to commands in French. Otherwise he has to translate, and that slows him down.

JOHN STEINBECK, *TRAVELS WITH CHARLEY*

There is no faith which has never yet been broken except that of a truly faithful dog.

KONRAD LORENZ, *KING SOLOMON'S RING*

The only dog I ever knew which died of a broken heart was an Irish terrier male that we had to send away from us one winter that we spent in apartments. Poor Badger, shall I ever forget the deep trouble in your hazel eyes, as we put you into the crate? And yet you trusted us, sat quietly while the slats were being hammered into place, went away without outcry.

MAZO DE LA ROCHE, *PORTRAIT OF A DOG*

I grew up to be an anonymous yellow cur looking like a cross between an Angora cat and a box of lemons.

O. HENRY, "MEMOIRS OF A YELLOW DOG"

FOOVIEW (foo' view) n. The ability of a dog to inflict guilt from any angle in the room while he watches his master eat.

RICH HALL, *SNIGLETS*

Every dog should have a man of his own. There is nothing like a well-behaved person around the house to spread the dog's blanket for him, or bring him his supper when he comes home man-tired at night.

COREY FORD, "EVERY DOG SHOULD HAVE A MAN"

We are alone, absolutely alone on this chance planet; and amid all the forms of life that surround us, not one, excepting the dog, has made an alliance with us.

MAURICE MAETERLINCK, "OUR FRIEND, THE DOG"

It may be weak of me, but a man has only to speak to me, and a sort of thrill goes right down my spine and sets my tail wagging.

P. G. WODEHOUSE, *A VERY SHY GENTLEMAN*

I've seen a look in dogs' eyes, a quickly vanishing look of amazed contempt, and I am convinced that dogs think humans are nuts.

JOHN STEINBECK, *TRAVELS WITH CHARLEY*

Not the least hard thing to bear when they go from us, these quiet friends, is that they carry away with them so many years of our own lives. Yet, if they find warmth therein, who would grudge them those years that they have so guarded? Nothing else of us can they take to lie upon with outstretched paws and chin stretched to the ground; and, whatever they take, be sure they have deserved.

JOHN GALSWORTHY, "MEMORIES"

I think we are drawn to dogs because they are the uninhibited creatures we might be if we weren't certain we knew better.

GEORGE BIRD EVANS, "TROUBLES WITH BIRD DOGS"

Man is troubled by what might be called the Dog Wish, a strange and involved compulsion to be as happy and carefree as a dog.

JAMES THURBER, "AND SO TO MEDVE"

Nobody can fully understand the meaning of love unless he's owned a dog. He can show you more honest affection with a flick of his tail than a man can gather through a lifetime of handshakes.

GENE HILL, "THE DOG MAN"

It is quite wrong to attempt to instill obedience into a dog by punishment and equally senseless to beat him afterwards when, enticed by the scent of some game, he has run away during a walk. The beating will cure him not of running away, which lies farther back in his memory, but probably of the coming back, with which he will assuredly connect the punishment.

KONRAD LORENZ, MAN MEETS DOG

We are to listen to a dog until we discover what is needed instead of imposing ourselves in the name of training.

THE MONKS OF NEW SKETE,
HOW TO BE YOUR DOG'S BEST FRIEND

I can't think of anything that brings me closer to tears than when my old dog—completely exhausted after a full and hard day in the field—limps away from her nice spot in front of the fire and comes over to where I'm sitting and puts her head in my lap, a paw over my knee and closes her eyes and goes back to sleep. I don't know what I've done to deserve that kind of friend.

GENE HILL, "THE DOG MAN"

Most dogs are earnest, which is why most people like them. You can say any fool thing to a dog, and the dog will give you this look that says, "My God, you're RIGHT! I NEVER would have thought of that!"

DAVE BARRY, "EARNING A COLLIE DEGREE"

Having once been punished, dogs remember, but like children, they hope they won't be caught in the act.

BARBARA WOODHOUSE, *NO BAD DOGS, THE WOODHOUSE WAY*

Business meetings, love meetings. Through fog, through snow, through mud, during biting dog-days, in streaming rain, they go, they come, they trot, they slip under carriages, urged on by fleas, passion, need, or duty. Like us, they get up early in the morning, and they seek their livelihood or pursue their pleasures.

CHARLES BAUDELAIRE, "THE PARISIAN PROWLER"

The old saw about old dogs and new tricks only applies to certain people.

DANIEL PINKWATER, "TRAIN YOUR DOG, DAMMIT!"

Canine cognomens should be designed to impinge on the ears of dogs and not to amuse neighbors, tradespeople, and casual visitors.

JAMES THURBER, "HOW TO NAME A DOG"

We have not to gain his confidence or his friendship: he is born our friend; while his eyes are still closed, already he believes in us: even before his birth, he has given himself to man.

MAURICE MAETERLINCK, "OUR FRIEND, THE DOG"

The great thing about dogs is, they never have attitude.

TOM GLIATTO ON MAX, THE JACK RUSSELL TERRIER
FEATURED IN *THE MASK, PEOPLE*

They have all the compactness of a small dog and all the valor of a big one. And they are so exceedingly sturdy that it is proverbial that the only thing fatal to them is being run over by an automobile—in which case the car itself knows that it has been in a fight.

DOROTHY PARKER, ON SCOTTISH TERRIERS,
"TOWARD THE DOG DAYS"

Do not think it is cruel to keep a dog in a town flat. His happiness depends largely upon how much time you can spend with him and upon how often he may accompany you on an errand. He does not mind waiting for hours at your study door if he is finally rewarded by a ten minutes' walk at your side.

KONRAD LORENZ, *KING SOLOMON'S RING*

I could never take dogs for granted. . . . They were just animals, after all, and it seemed to me that their main preoccupation ought to be in seeking food and protection; instead they dispensed a flow of affection and loyalty which appeared to be limitless.

JAMES HERRIOT, *JAMES HERRIOT'S DOG STORIES*

Once a great hunting dog, today the Cocker is useless in the field. It can't hunt its way to the meat counter in a supermarket.

RICHARD A. WOLTERS, *DUCK DOGS*

A really companionable and indispensable dog is an accident of nature. You can't get it by breeding for it, and you can't buy it with money. It just happens along.

E. B. WHITE, "THE CARE AND TRAINING OF A DOG"

Index